# 10217

# THE THREE BEARS
# RHYME BOOK

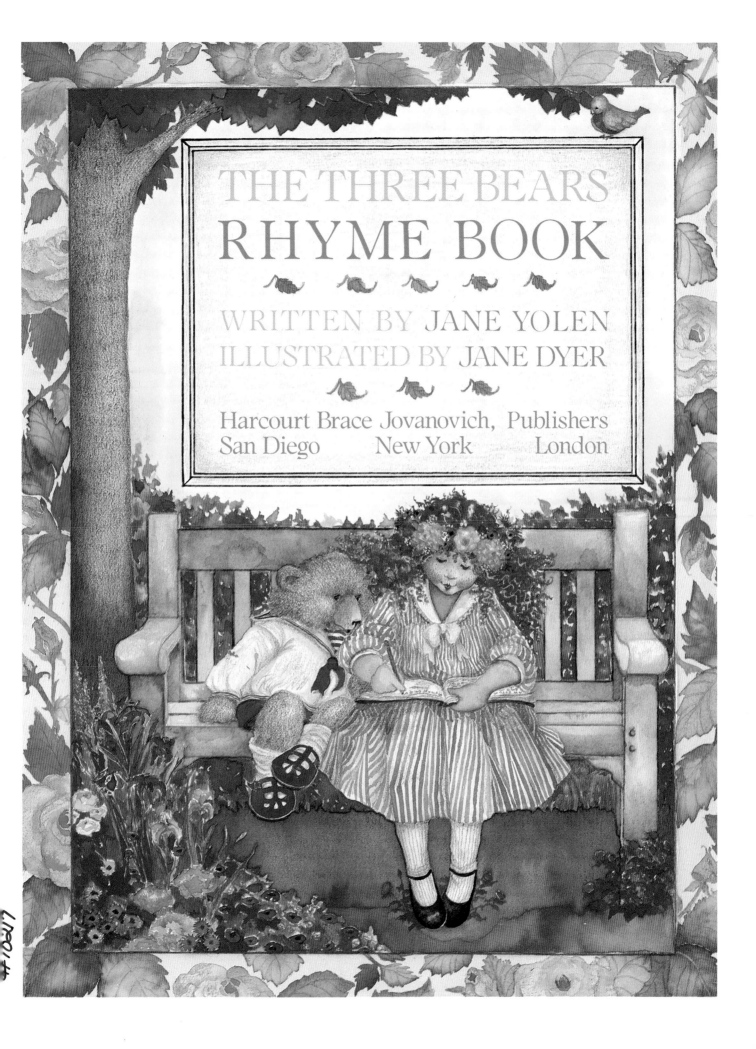

# THE THREE BEARS
# RHYME BOOK

WRITTEN BY JANE YOLEN
ILLUSTRATED BY JANE DYER

Harcourt Brace Jovanovich, Publishers
San Diego          New York          London

For Lui, who waltzes with bears
—J. Y.
To my mother, who first taught me to draw
—J. D.

Requests for permission to make copies of any part of the work should be mailed to:
Permissions, Harcourt Brace Jovanovich, Publishers, Orlando, Florida 32887.

Library of Congress Cataloging-in-Publication Data
Yolen, Jane.
The three bears rhyme book.
Summary: Fifteen poems portray three familiar bears
and their friend Goldie engaged in such activities as
taking a walk, eating porridge, and having a birthday party.
1. Bears—Juvenile poetry. 2. Children's poetry,
American. [1. Bears—Poetry. 2. American poetry]
I. Dyer, Jane, ill. II. Three bears. III. Title.
PS3575.043T47 1987    811'.54    86-19514
ISBN 0-15-286386-9

Printed in the United States of America

First edition

A  B  C  D  E

The illustrations in this book were done in colored pencils and Dr. Martin's
watercolors on 140-lb. Fabriano hot press watercolor paper.
The text type was set in Adroit Light by Central Graphics, San Diego, California.
The display type was set in Adroit Light by Thompson Type, San Diego, California.
Color separations were made by Heinz Weber, Inc., Los Angeles, California.
Printed and bound by Horowitz/Rae
Book Manufacturers, Inc., Fairfield, New Jersey
Designed by Dalia Hartman
Production supervision by Warren Wallerstein and Rebecca Miller

# CONTENTS

 **PORRIDGE**

There are always three bowls,
And always three spoons,
And Momma Bear humming
Her wake-me-up tunes.

There are always three napkins,
Always three chairs,
And the great big yawns
Of breakfasting bears.

As far or as old
As I grow to be,
That's what porridge
Will mean to me.

# THREE BEARS WALKING

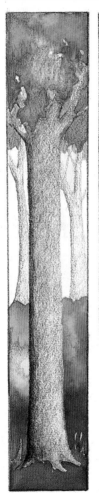

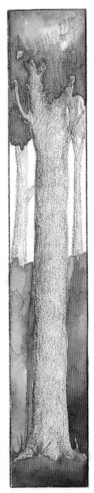

Three bears walking
down the lane, down the lane.
Three bears talking,
"Do you think it's going to rain?"
Three bears walking
to the wood, to the wood.
Three bears talking,
"Pretty day!" "Pretty good!"
Three bears walking
under trees, under trees.
Three bears talking,
"Do you know where there are bees?"
Three bears walking
by a stream, by a stream.
Three bears talking,
"Pass the berries." "Pass the cream."
Three bears walking
to their den, to their den.
Three bears talking,
"Great to be back home again."

# BOUQUET

In Goldie's garden,
flowers grow
within a neat
and ordered row.

But in our woodland,
never neat,
grow jumbled rose
and meadowsweet,

and lily bell
and Queen Anne's lace
and dandelions
every place.

Now, I prefer
the wildness where
the flowers have
to give and share.

But Goldie says
both things are good:
the well-kept garden
*and* the wood.

RAIN

It's not much fun being out in the rain,
Without rubber boots, red rubber boots.
I'll say it LOUD and I'll say it plain:
It's not much fun being out in the rain
With the drops running down my fur like a drain,
And these words in my head like an old refrain:
It's not much fun being out in the rain
Without some bright new red rubber boots.

It's not much fun being out in the rain
Without an umbrella, a red umbrella.
It's not much fun, so I think I'll explain
That it's not much fun being out in the rain
With the drops on my nose like beads on a chain.
So I'll sit in a puddle and pout and complain
That it's not much fun being out in the rain
Without a brand-new red umbrella.

It's not much fun being out in the rain
Without a slicker, a yellow slicker.
It's not much fun, so I'll say it again
That my fur is soaked and will likely stain,
And that's why it's not much fun in the rain
And this song running 'round and 'round my brain:
It is not much fun being out in the rain
Without boots and a slicker and a red umbrella.

(Especially right before my birthday!)

# PHOTOGRAPHS

This is me in my first bed.
This is the back of Poppa's head.
This is Poppa's favorite mug.
This is Momma on a rug.
This is Goldie with the chair
You broke the day I wasn't there.

This is me. I'm eating—see.
This is me on Poppa's knee.
This is Momma holding Spot.
You think that this is me—it's not!
And here we are upon the stairs:
Goldilocks and all three bears.

# BEAR PARADE

I can hear the sound of their marching feet
And a great drumroll and a rat-a-tat beat
As the bears come marching down my street,
Singing *Hip Hip Hooray for Bears!*

There's a bear in red with a great big stick,
And a teddy bear with a honey lick,
And a hundred more who are stepping quick,
Singing *Hip Hip Hooray for Bears!*

# rat-a-tat, rat-a-tat

There's a bear with a bunch of bright balloons,
And a pair of bears playing big bassoons,
And they're shouting out their favorite tunes,
Singing *Hip Hip Hooray for Bears!*

Now you may prefer being out on the sea,
Or in front of a roaring fire with your tea,
But the bears' parade is the place for me,
Singing *Hip Hip Hooray for Bears!*

BIRTHDAY PARTY

Honeycakes and ice cream,
Blackberry pie,
Everybody singing
What a jolly bear am I.

A wish for every candle,
A present from each friend,
A great big hug from Goldie.
Why do birthdays have to end?

# TOO OLD
# FOR NAPS

I'm old enough
to wash my face.
I'm old enough
to set my place.
I'm old enough
to tie a lace.
And I'm much too old for naps.

I'm old enough
for no night-light.
I'm old enough
to bear-hug tight.
I know my left paw
from my right.
And I'm much too old for naps.

I'm old enough
to walk the lane
to Goldie's
even in the rain.
At bedtime—do I
still complain?
No!
  So I'm *much* too old for naps!

# WHEN A BEAR GETS MAD

When a bear gets mad
He gives a roar
And shows his teeth
And slams the door

And jumps in bed
And hides his eyes
And sometimes
(Very softly) cries.

But after, when
The mad is done,
A bear is ready
For some fun

And doesn't want
To think some more
About the teeth
And growl and roar,

But needs a hug
And wants a smile,
Which all will happen . . .
In a while.

# FINDING MY GROWL

Poppa says it's in my throat.
Momma says my teeth.
Granny says it's in my chest,
Just slightly underneath.

Goldie says that in my head
Is where my growl should be.
But Gramps says that my growl is hid
Deep down inside of me.

Gr . . . grr . . . grrr . . . grrrrrrrowl.

# BEARS'

Some bears sit
in great big chairs,
great big chairs
for great big bears,
great big legs
and claws on feet,
great big pillows,
great big seat.

Some bears sit
in middling chairs,
middling chairs
for middling bears.
Rockers make
the chair a ship
for bears who like
to take a trip.

# CHAIRS

Some bears sit
in tiny chairs,
tiny chairs
for tiny bears.
Tiny chairs
can be quite tall
with straps so
baby bear won't fall.

But of all bears' chairs,
the very best
is to lie against
your poppa's chest
and cuddle up
to take a nap
upon the chair
that's Poppa's lap.

25

# HOW TO BATHE
## A BEAR

1. Be sure the water's warm.
2. The bubbles fill the tub.
3. The rubber duck is there.
4. Find bear cub.

5. And quickly mop the floor.
6. Say: "Don't forget to scrub."
7. Feel for plug—and pull.
8. Dry bear cub.

READ TO ME

Read to me riddles
and read to me rhymes,
read to me stories
of magical times.

Read to me tales
about castles and kings,
read to me stories
of fabulous things.

Read to me pirates,
and read to me knights,
read to me dragons
and dragon-back flights.

Read to me spaceships
and cowboys and then
when you are finished—
please read them again!

Goldie says
there are monsters in the night,
and they hide in your closet
till you turn off the light.
Then they howl and growl
just to let you know they're there.
But I'm not afraid
                              because
I'm a big bear.

Goldie says
that underneath my bed
there are ghosts that are people
who are not quite dead,
and a skeleton sits
in my rocking chair.
But I'm not afraid
                              because
I'm a big bear.

Goldie says
there's a vampire bat
and a vampire bullfrog
and a vampire cat
just waiting to jump
and to give me quite a scare.
But I'm not afraid
                              because
I'm a big bear.

But just in case
that Goldie may be right,
would you be awfully mad
if I left on my light?
If I slept in your bed
would you really really care?
I know YOU'RE not afraid,
                              you're
a great BIG bear.

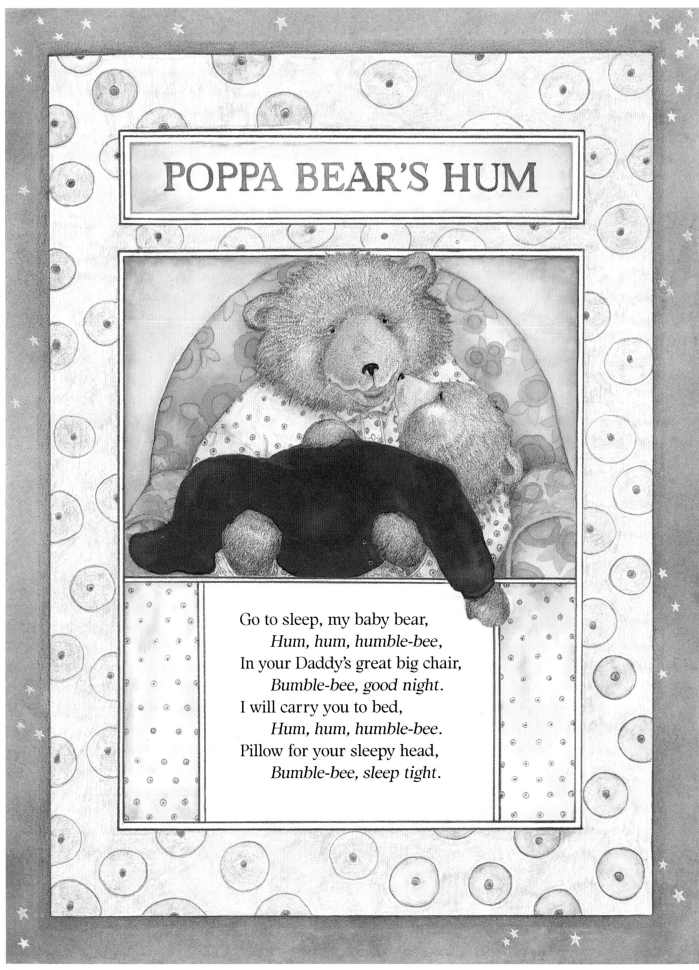

# POPPA BEAR'S HUM

Go to sleep, my baby bear,
*Hum, hum, humble-bee,*
In your Daddy's great big chair,
*Bumble-bee, good night.*
I will carry you to bed,
*Hum, hum, humble-bee.*
Pillow for your sleepy head,
*Bumble-bee, sleep tight.*